W9-AYO-552

Help Me **Understand**

Why Do My Parents Fight?

Melissa Raé Shofner

PowerKiDS press™

NEW YORK

Published in 2019 by The Rosen Publishing Group, Inc.
29 East 21st Street, New York, NY 10010

Copyright © 2019 by The Rosen Publishing Group, Inc.

All rights reserved. No part of this book may be reproduced in any form without permission in writing from the publisher, except by a reviewer.

First Edition

Editor: Elizabeth Krajnik
Book Design: Rachel Rising

Photo Credits: Cover, g-stockstudio/Shutterstock.com; p. 4 pimchawee/Shutterstock.com; pp. 5, 13, 15 wavebreakmedia/Shutterstock.com; p. 6 Littlekidmoment/Shutterstock.com; p. 7 David Pereiras/Shutterstock.com; p. 9 PhotoMediaGroup/Shutterstock.com; p. 10 Dmitry A/Shutterstock.com; p. 11 Paparacy/Shutterstock.com; p. 16 Irina Bg/Shutterstock.com; p. Monkey Business Images/Shutterstock.com; p. 18 © iStockphoto/princessdlaf; p. 19 Firma V/Shutterstock.com; p. 20 Brian A Jackson/Shutterstock.com; p. 21 fizkes/Shutterstock.com; p. 22 Rob Marmion/Shutterstock.com.

Cataloging-in-Publication Data

Names: Shofner, Melissa Raé.
Title: Why do my parents fight? / Melissa Raé Shofner.
Description: New York : PowerKids Press, 2019. | Series: Help me understand | Includes glossary and index.
Identifiers: LCCN ISBN 9781508167280 (pbk.) | ISBN 9781508167266 (library bound) | ISBN 9781508167297 (6 pack)
Subjects: LCSH: Families–Juvenile literature. | Interpersonal conflict–Juvenile literature. | Family violence–Juvenile literature. | Divorce–Juvenile literature.
Classification: LCC HQ744.S5345 2019 | DDC 306.85–dc23

Manufactured in the United States of America

CPSIA Compliance Information: Batch #CS18PK: For Further Information contact Rosen Publishing, New York, New York at 1-800-237-9932

Contents

Everybody Argues

Everybody gets into disagreements now and then. They're just a part of life. You can't agree with other people about everything all the time. Sometimes these disagreements turn into **arguments**. Arguments can actually be good, as long as the people **involved** are being truthful and understanding of each other's thoughts and feelings.

Unfortunately, many people end up fighting instead of arguing. During a fight, people might yell and say mean things to each other. People fight for many reasons, but it never helps them fix their problems.

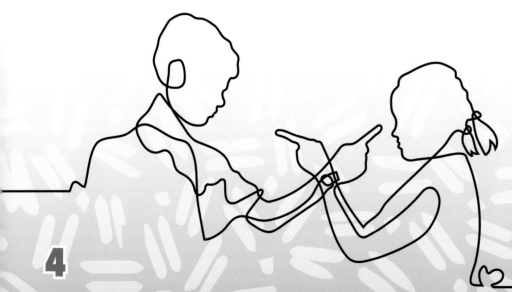

An argument gives both people a chance to speak and be heard. A fight does not.

5

Why Adults Might Fight

You've probably been in a fight with a friend or your brother or sister. Adults get into fights, too. Maybe your parents fight sometimes. This can be scary and **confusing**, especially if you don't understand what they're fighting about.

Having jobs, owning a home, and raising a family aren't easy. Parents might not always agree on how they should spend their time or money. Disagreements over these things sometimes lead to fights. Always remember that if your parents fight, it's never your **fault**.

Money is one of the biggest reasons adults fight. Sometimes parents don't agree on how they should spend their money.

Sometimes one parent might feel like they're doing more work around the house than the other parent. Maybe your dad does yard work all weekend while your mom goes shopping. Or maybe your mom always stays home with you and your baby sister while your dad goes golfing with his friends.

People often fight when they don't feel equal. Finding a **balance** can be hard for parents because they have so many responsibilities. Not everyone is good at talking about their problems.

Responsibilities are tasks that you're expected or required to do. Parents have many responsibilities, such as going to work, feeding their children, and cleaning their home.

Making It Worse

Fights happen for many reasons. There are also many things that can make them worse. Your parents have many responsibilities that may create **stress** for them. Working long hours can be stressful. Coming home to a messy house can be stressful. If one of your parents isn't feeling well, that can be stressful, too.

For some people, fighting is a way to let off steam at the end of a long, hard day. This doesn't make it OK, though. There are better ways to get rid of stress.

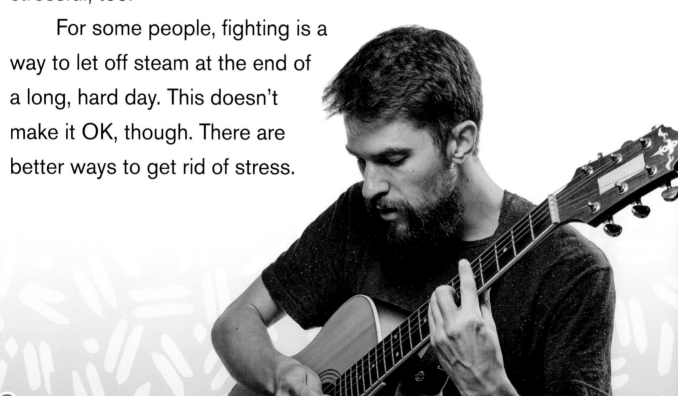

You might play a school sport or take music lessons. It's important for parents to have hobbies, or activities they enjoy, too. Hobbies give parents a healthy way to deal with stress.

Feeling Unsafe

When your parents fight, they might get upset and yell, cry, or even scream at each other. They might say hurtful things they don't mean or call each other names. During a bad fight, they might throw or break objects around your home.

You might feel unsafe if your parents fight like this. Stay out of their way when they're fighting. If you're scared or worried about your safety or your parents' safety, you should call another trusted adult as soon as you can.

One of your parents might try to control and hold power over the other parent. They might also hurt the other parent on purpose. This is called domestic violence. You should tell a trusted adult if this happens.

The Silent Treatment

When someone gives you the "silent treatment," it means they're ignoring you, or pretending not to hear or see you, because they're angry. It might not seem like your parents are fighting when they give each other the silent treatment, but they are.

The silent treatment happens when your parents are mad and don't know how to share their thoughts and feelings with each other. It might make you sad or worried to know your parents aren't talking, but remember—it's not your fault.

Your parents might stop talking to each other after a big, loud fight. You may want to help, but it's not a good idea to get in the middle of a silent fight, either.

Finding Help

Hearing or seeing your parents fight can leave you with many emotions, or strong feelings. You might be scared if you hear your parents yell. If you don't understand why they're fighting, you might feel confused. You may worry that your parents don't love you or each other.

No matter what emotions you have, you shouldn't be afraid to talk to a trusted adult. This might be your grandparent, your aunt or uncle, or one of your teachers at school.

Talking to a trusted adult can make you feel better. If the fighting gets out of hand, they can help you feel safe and find help for you and your family.

17

What You Can Do

If your parents are fighting about something that has to do with you, you might feel **guilty**. Remember, though, the reasons they're fighting are not your fault. Even though you can't fix your parents' problems or stop the fights, you can find ways to deal with your feelings.

It's a good idea to stay out of the way during a fight. Go in your room and read or listen to music. Try not to worry. Most fights will pass in time. If not, think about talking to another adult.

Getting your homework done and doing your chores without being asked will also help your parents be less stressed.

Understanding Divorce

When parents fight, they might try to fix their problems by talking to someone called a therapist. Therapists are good listeners who can help people talk through their problems and find ways to fix them.

Sometimes, however, parents might decide that it's better for them and their family if they divorce, or stop being married to each other. If your parents get divorced, it doesn't mean they don't love you or each other anymore. They're just trying to do what's best for everyone.

Divorce is hard on everyone involved. Sometimes even divorce doesn't keep parents from fighting. Just know that you're not to blame for this.

21

Always Loved

It's not easy to live with parents who fight all the time. It can make you sad or worried. You may not understand the reasons for the fighting. You might feel like it's your fault, even though it isn't.

Everyone argues sometimes, but fighting doesn't help fix problems. If you ever feel scared when your parents are fighting, don't be afraid to talk to an adult you trust. There are many people, including your parents, who love you very much and want you to feel safe.

Glossary

argument: An angry disagreement.

balance: A state in which different things happen in equal amounts.

confusing: Causing confusion, or a state of unclarity or uncertainty.

fault: Responsibility for a problem or mistake.

guilty: Feeling bad because you believe you did something bad or wrong.

involve: To have or include someone or something as a part of something.

stress: Strong feelings of worry caused by problems in your life or work.

Index

Websites

Due to the changing nature of Internet links, PowerKids Press has developed an online list of websites related to the subject of this book. This site is updated regularly. Please use this link to access the list: www.powerkidslinks.com/help/fight